MODELLING POSTWAR TANKS

Osprey Modelling Manuals
Volume 10

Publication Manager: Rodrigo Hernandez Cabos

Series Editor: Jerry Scutts

OSPREY

1

Osprey Modelling Manuals 10

MODELLING POSTWAR TANKS

First published in Great Britain in 2000 by Osprey Publishing, Elms Court, Chapel Way, Botley, Oxford OX2 9LP, United Kingdom.
Email: info@ospreypublishing.com

© Accion Press, S. A., C/Ezequiel Solana, 16, 28017, Madrid, Spain.
  Euro Modelismo 1992

ISBN 1 84176 138 9

English edition packaged by Compendium, 1st Floor, 43 Frith Street, London, W1V 5TE

00 01 02 03 04   10 9 8 7 6 5 4 3 2 1

Publication Manager: Rodrigo Hernández Cabos
Photographs: Salvador Gómez Mico, Rodrigo Hernández Cabos, Aurelio Gimeno
Modelling Team: Sergio de Usera Múgica, Cristóbal Vergara Durán, Rodrigo Hernández Cabos, Pedro Andrada, Miguel Jimenez Martín, José A. Velázquez Encinas, Luis Palencia, José Borrachero Sánchez

Printed in Spain

For a catalogue of all books published by Osprey Military, Automotive and Aviation please contact:

**The Marketing Manager, Osprey Direct UK, PO Box 140, Wellingborough, Northants, NN8 4ZA, United Kingdom.
Tel. (0)1933 443863, Fax (0)1933 443849.
Email: info@ospreydirect.co.uk**

**The Marketing Manager, Osprey Direct USA, PO Box 130, Sterling Heights, MI 48311-0130, USA.
Tel. 248 399 6191, Fax 248 399 6194. Email: info@ospreydirectusa.com**

Visit Osprey at:
www.ospreypublishing.com

INTRODUCTION

This is the tenth in Osprey's Modelling Manuals series and the fourth on tanks — the response to a demand for detail on the extremely difficult art of modelling armoured fighting vehicles. This book looks at the early postwar vehicles, some of which had seen action in northwest Europe in World War II, but most of which were developed or modified to keep pace with the technology of the modern era.

To anyone who has studied the postwar areas of action — Korea, Vietnam, the Arab–Israeli wars, Afghanistan — the vehicles here need little introduction; for those who have not studied their AFV history, the vehicles in this book will prove every bit as interesting. The Soviet Bloc is well represented with coverage of:

• the **T-34/85**, a classic WWII AFV, this one seen in Croatia in the modern period with substantial detail on ersatz camouflage patterns (pages 56–60).

• the **T-54 Model 1951** is seen in Central Front 1960s' camouflage when the Cold War was at its height and it wasn't a matter of if they come, just when. This model is a conversion of a T-55 kit (pages 4–9).

• the **T-62 BDD** seen as modified in the field in Afghanistan, with substantial appliqué armour and wire screens to reduce possible damage from RPGs (pages 49–55).

The Western Allies are represented by an interesting range of vehicles:

• Sweden's **Strv-103 S-Tank**, the turretless tank developed in the 1960s (pages 10–18).

• the US **M60** gets coverage in its modern A1 RISE and Blazer forms, with reactive armour giving the vehicles a bizarre form (pages 29–39).

• the **M551 Sheridan** is modified to show its Vietnam persona, complete with commander's machine gun protection (pages 19–28).

• two US mobile artillery pieces are covered to broaden the AFV spectrum — the **M41** and **M43** (pages 40–44 and 45–48).

• **Merkava**, Israel's home-grown MBT shows the difficulties associated with painting realistic desert wear and tear (pages 60–64)

T-54 Model 1951

As an injection-moulded model of the T-54 does not exist on the market, the starting point for this conversion was the Esci T-55 kit.

The fuel cans were based on one from the Tamiya T-62 kit. After modification, resin copies were made.

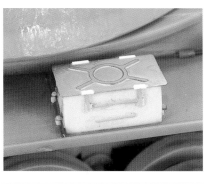

The small box is made of plastic, with an etched-brass lid from the Todo Modelismo accessory kit.

This Italian kit has good detailing, although there are some errors with the shape which we will correct in due course. We used the MB T-54A resin conversion kit to modify the turret and barrel, and we also used the etched-brass On The Mark Model T-54/T-55 conversion kit and plate no. 5 from Todo Modelismo.

Conversion is not an easy task for beginners, it takes time to learn the necessary skills —

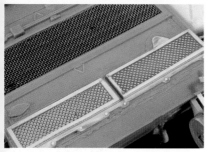

Reworking the engine grilles is an important detail that improves the appearance of the model.

Added details on the upper glacis plate.

View of the box on the left side: it has been copied in resin and improved with etched-brass details.

such as scratch-building some pieces, preparing resin moulds, etc. But these are skills that it is important to learn: without them your model-making world will be a lot smaller and a great deal duller.

This chapter looks at the creation of a T-54 Model 1951, but with some more modern details, such as the wheels, headlights, supplementary fuel tanks, etc.

The job starts with the upper hull of the tank — more specifically with the engine

Note the large amount of extra detailing that must be added to the back of the turret.

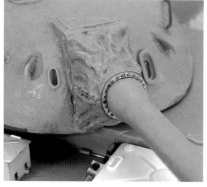

Additional gun mantlet detailing.

the smoke canisters were scratch-built from pieces of plastic card.

grids. Eliminate the moulded plastic piece, which is divided in two, and put in its place a more realistic fine grid. Further towards the back of the tank, make two more new grids with plastic sheet and mosquito net.

Once this is finished, the hull can be assembled, but the side skirts must be left clean so that the tool boxes and fuel tanks will fit onto them. Unfortunately, the rectangular fuel tanks provided on the model are wrong — each is a different size, when in reality all three were identical. To resolve this, we used a Tamiya T-62 fuel tank. It had to be modified slightly, since it had two bevels on the corners, when those on the T-54 only have one. Once we had produced one accurate fuel tank, two others were made from a silicone mould. We did the same thing with the two tool boxes, using the Verlinden T-55 resin kit as the basis. To get the detailing right (the design is different on the upper part of the T-54), we added an etched-brass piece from the Todo Modelismo set.

The small holes made to insert the copper wire are concealed by putty.

The left-hand side is completed with another plastic can.

On the other skirt (right) there is a small box measuring 13.5mm x 5.5mm, which has to be made using 1mm plastic sheet, although its top is included in the Todo Modelismo set. All the angle bars that hold down the skirts are added later (they come from the On the Mark kit).

The plastic piece at the rear of these skirts is curved. This is inaccurate, because although it has a small curved area, it terminates in a straight area. There is no alternative but to reconstruct it completely in 0.5mm plastic. Finally, we had to add a pair of cylindrical smoke canisters to the rear of the vehicle. These were made from scratch from plastic sheet.

The front headlights are made of resin, with grilles and wiring made from copper wire.

It is also necessary to rework the turret grab rails using with thick copper wire. At the back of the turret, more U-shaped wire pieces are added (see photo at top left page 6), plus a number of lights and bits of ironwork.

Also, both cupolas lack details such as periscopes, tops, etc, all of which are made of plastic.

The gun barrel has recently come onto the market and is the one included in the Jordí Rubio resin kit, but it is made of turned aluminium.

Some edges are highlighted with a metallic colour to show wear.

Dry-brush painting emphasises the rear engine grilles.

PAINTING

The colour scheme chosen for this model is that of the Soviet Army of the mid-1960s — a typical green covering the whole tank. The colour used is Russian green (M-114 from Humbrol) with a little black. Once dried, we painted on the first dry brush layer with the same colour but without darkening. Later, to highlight details, another dry brush layer was applied using light green (M-151 Humbrol).

We started by painting the tracks black, then later used gun metal (M-53) to give a rust-coloured wash. Finally, the last details were brought out with aluminium (M-56). The tracks were then installed on the wheels following the kit instructions, although, as can be seen in the photos, the upper section has been bent slightly to produce a soft curve which gives it a more realistic appearance.

At the rear of the turret, a tarpaulin was made from a paper handkerchief. This was painted brown (M-156), then made paler with light earth (M-119). The belts are black (M-33).

The tactical numbering transfers are from Verlinden 'Soviet vehicle numbers' No 488. For the ageing process, oil was washed over the hatches; and the back and glacis areas were coloured mainly with sienna, brown and even pale grey. The tank's episcopes were painted RAF blue (M-9), with light touches of medium blue (M-59) at the centre.

Around the exhausts, the engine grid and the rear of the turret, Tamiya smoke grey has been applied using an airbrush. Sepia and brown inks were applied to the lower area. Finally the entire model was covered with Marabú matt varnish — with the exception of the episcopes and headlights, where we used gloss varnish.

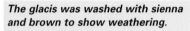
Tactical markings are from a Verlinden decals set.

The glacis was washed with sienna and brown to show weathering.

Around the exhausts Tamiya smoke grey was applied by airbrush.

S-TANK

The Strv-103 turretless tank was designed by AB Bofors to reduce the height, and therefore the vulnerability, of the Swedish Army's main battle tank.

This remarkable tank has been almost entirely forgotten by manufacturers. The British company Accurate Armour is one of the few to have produced an S-Tank model. The kit in question is made of resin, or rather what today is defined as 'multimedia' — a mixture of resin, lead and etched brass. The quality of the kit is superb with a great deal of good moulded detail. The cost of the kit reflects this quality and range of materials used. However, despite these positive points, there are drawbacks. First, there are no decals or transfers included. Second, although the assembly sequence is explained well, the instructions lack any painting outline. Finally, some resin parts have bubbles (very few) or a little mould displacement.

Although the assembly does not take very long, it is complicated and consequently this type of kit is not recommended for beginners. For example, the model in question arrived with the area of the driver's roof concave. To put this right, it needed the help of hot air from a hair drier applied to the area; with a little pressure the fault was easily corrected.

Etched brass detailing.

Other examples are that, when joining the rear section, the join must not be levelled, but rather overlap by approximately one millimetre. Easily the most problematic section is the assembly of the lead wheel axles, since they must be perfectly aligned. The best way to do this is to mount the resin on a plastic support, made to the right height: we stuck the resin on this support with adhesive tape and added the axles one by one.

Note that it is better to paint some pieces — such as the side-skirts, wheels, commander's cupola and the dozer blades — separately and mount them at the end. The etched-brass pieces must be joined firmly to the hull using cyanoacrylate glue.

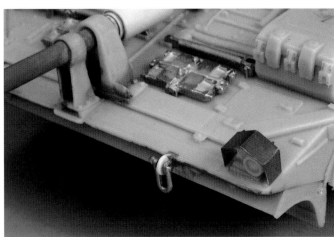

PAINTING

Perhaps the most attractive feature of the tank is the geometric camouflage in four colours. As already mentioned, Accurate do not include any painting guide in the modelling outline, so the colours and their distribution have been taken from a couple of rare photos of the actual tank, and it is must be emphasised that finding documentation on the Model C is very difficult.

For the painting Russian green (M-114 from Humbrol) is used as the base colour. Similarly, the skirts and wheels are entirely this same colour. The camouflage is laid down in stages, masking off each colour part in turn. On the base we then applied a khaki colour, produced by mixing 70 percent khaki drill (M-72) and 30 percent French artiller' green (M-179). Next we masked the khaki colour and applied the brown (M-186). To finish, we used black green (M-91). On each colour we used a dry-brush technique to lighten the respective tone with matt white paint. Some pieces (such as the smoke mortars, or the flexible extension to the exhaust pipe) were painted olive drab (M-66). The mortar projectile containers, located on the driver's hatch, are 70 percent dark grey (M-156) and 30 percent RAF blue (M-96). For the interior of the periscopes, a mixture of 50 percent grass green (M-80) and medium blue (M-89) is used. The anti-skid rectangles are

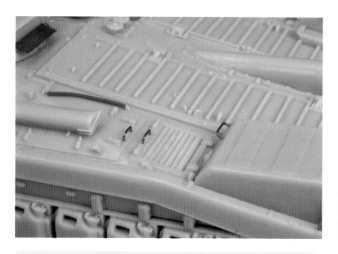

Fine copper wire is ideal for reproducing small handgrips, rings, etc.

The commander's cupola and machine gun assembly are among the most delicate and difficult parts to model. Nevertheless, they provide magnificent detail.

Details of the rear decking.

Additional plastic tubing provides the correct barrel thickness.

The white metal pieces are also of good quality and easy to work.

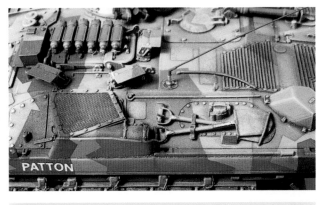

Painting doesn't hide the quality of detail on this splendid model.

The famous name and numbers on the sides are transfers (decals).

surface grey (M-162). With a very light airbrushing of sepia or dark brown ink, we dirtied the lower areas of the tank. Then, with the colour smoke (X-19 from Tamiya) we gave a smoky tone to the engine grids.

The numbers belong to a Japanese aeroplane kit and are at 1/72 scale. The yellow squares on black are made with clean tracing paper of the same colour,

Rear decking after painting.

are the small orange reflective rectangles. Using black and aviation yellow, stencil lettering is placed as shown in the photos.

The tactical name 'Patton' is produced from Letraset. To finish, the entire model is covered with matt varnish except for the periscopes and lights, which are gloss finished.

The front boxes have three anti-slip bands on their upper surfaces, which have been painted grey.

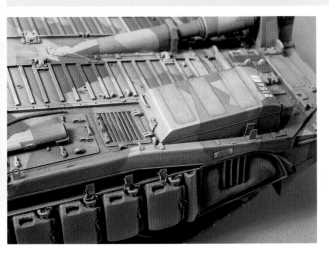

Anti-slip bands are also noticeable at the rear.

Commander's hatch and interior detail. (photo Saumur Museum)

The right camouflage scheme helps emphasise the great quality of this model.

Right: The radio operator's seat faces backwards. (photo Saumur Museum)

Below Right: The lower part of the side skirts are painted with dust effects.

Bottom Right: Commander's cupola, details of the machine gun and containers for the smoke discharger ammunition; the latter are painted bluish-grey.

15

An examination of a full-size example of the vehicle you want to model gives you a better feel for the subject and an eye for detail.

The design of the 'S' tank or Stridvagn 103, was begun in the early 1950s when Sweden, a country with a great military and arms' manufacturing tradition, issued a series of requirements for companies to tender for the construction of a nationally produced combat tank. The winner was the internationally renowned Bofors company, whose 1958 design adopted a turretless vehicle, with the gun mounted on the chassis along the lines of the German tank destroyers of World War II. During 1961 the first two prototypes were completed for evaluation and they incorporated key technological advances.

The first thing to note is that the crew of the S-Tank is only two — the 105mm cannon has an automatic loader for 50 projectiles — and this makes a loader unnecessary (although whether this automatic loader is sufficiently reliable is debatable). The maximum rate of fire is 15 shots per minute, and the range

Top view of one of the two rear equipment boxes.

Rear light detail.

reliably while it is moving and cannot maintrain an alignment on an enemy vehicle while on the move. There has been an attempt to minimise this fact by using Bofors guns, but this is still a major tactical disadvantage, which is not compensated for by its low silhouette. In fact, the low silhouette is more perceived than real since it measures barely 20cm less in height than, for example, a Russian T-72. All these factors mean that the S-Tank is little more than a mobile anti-tank gun.

It is, nevertheless, a perfect vehicle for ambushing given the advantages of its profile and the type of terrain in which it operates. It has good first strike survivability and its two engines minimise the risk of the S-Tank being immobilised by an engineering fault.

propel itself in water at 6km/h; as well as having a new type of turbine. The last model produced was the Type C, whose main difference is the installation of a pair of mortars, a new flotation system and a front bulldozer blade, which has become standard on all these tanks.

The biggest problem with this vehicle is that it cannot shoot

of ammunition carried includes APDS, HE and smoke. Another important characteristic of the S-Tank is the hydropneumatic suspension with independent axles, which gives the tank its aiming flexibility — a maximum elevation of 12° and a depression of up to -10°.

The tank has two engines; one of them a conventional 249hp engine used to travel on roads, while the second is a 490hp gas turbine used to move over uneven terrain.

The tests on the first vehicles continued until 1967, the year in which the first series-produced versions, named S-Tank Type A, were delivered; the Swedish army changed this denomination to Strv-103A.

The Model B very soon began production; this was different from the previous tank as it incorporated a flotation and fording system to enable it to

Front head light and tow hook detail.

Support for the extinguisher located on the right side.

View of rear decking and engine ventilation grilles.

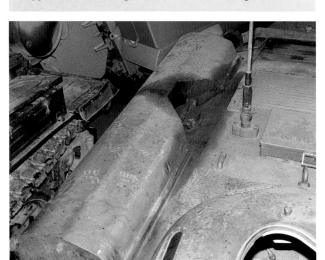

Exhaust pipe detail.

Detail of the driver's periscope.

View down the barrel and of the glacis plate: note the non-slip bands.

M551 SHERIDAN
Superdetailing, Construction and Painting

The role of the M551 Sheridan light tank was to cover the immediate fire support needs of airborne forces. It was specially designed to be dropped by parachute into the target area.

There are some scale models that are a really stimulating challenge for the model maker, because they have unique aspects of particular interest. The Sheridan light tank is one of these, as it is a rarely seen model and the model maker needs to contribute a lot of skill to improve it. The pieces that need to be superdetailed are easy enough to construct, especially when you consider the large amount of material that is available through Evergreen, so the task is an enjoyable one and the tank, once completed, is very pleasing — one of those satisfying models that produce the feeling that the madel maker has done a great deal more than simply a straightforward assembly.

For the documentation, we used only two publications, both from Squadron Signal Publications: *Armor in Vietnam* and *M-551 Sheridan*, both by the Jim Nesko.

It is best to divide up the work into separate sections: turret, hull, suspension system, and so on. We started with the turret. The first thing to be worked on is the set that forms the commander's mobile hatch with periscope and the ring that covers them, which is a decagon in shape externally but circular internally. Although it is rather thick, it must be made using $\frac{3}{10}$mm thick plastic. For this we first prepared a circle with the

The commander's hatch and cupola is reconstructed with plastic sheet and wire of different thicknesses.

The external profile of the cupola ring has ten sides.

It is important to choose the correct thickness of plastic sheet for each piece.

The armour plate surrounds are made of 0.5mm sheet completed with copper wire.

To improve the springs, the originals have been replaced with wire wound around a pin and cut to length.

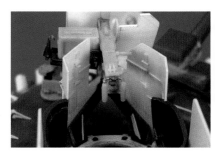

The connectors for the different armour plates were made by cutting plastic strips to length.

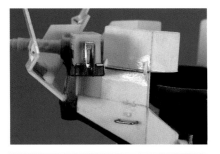

The .50 cal machine gun comes from a Verlinden resin kit.

The rear door opens with a device made of copper wire.

This type of protective armour was often added in Vietnam.

As the armour is flat it is easy to make, although it is a good idea to do it on paper first.

Note the rear carrying basket. The metal grid is imitated with Verlinden synthetic mesh.

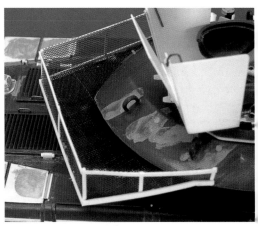

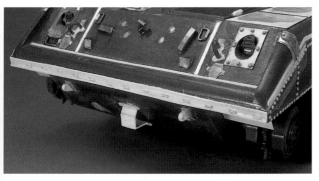
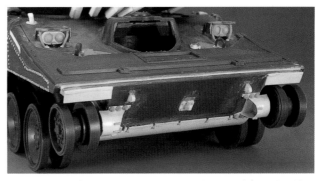

exterior diameter, tracing the spokes to obtain the ten sides, which were cut with a knife; then the interior was cut with a cutting compass, the external borders were reduced to size using sandpaper, then a series of large rivets were also added. Another ring must be placed on this first ring to support the hatch doors; this is made of the same thickness plastic, but is somewhat smaller and needs some tabs to anchor the doors. The support for the doors is made with sections of tube and copper wire for the spring, which is obtained by winding the metal around a nail or pin of an appropriate diameter. Finally, this part is completed with small pieces made with plastic strips.

The 0.50in. machine gun is surrounded by additional armour protection added in the field (similar to that used on the M113 for a period of time). Composed of a series of sheets of metal, they are made from 0.4mm plastic sheet, detailing grips and fasteners with copper wire. The machine gun is a resin and etched-brass kit by Verlinden.

The second hatchway on the left of the main cupola is improved by new hinges, strips of plastic and copper wire being used for the hinge and handle. The periscopes are modified by adding detail, and you need to prepare sockets for the infra-red headlights.

Another important element is the large, irregularly shaped turret bustle basket made up of a frame supporting wire netting.

It extends from the right-hand side just behind the commander's cupola around half the turret's circumference. This part was created using strips of Evergreen plastic and Verlinden netting.

Another characteristic feature of the M551 is the infra-red searchlight assembly — an M60 resin kit from Verlinden. The square forms of the kit were reshaped into an octagon by removing resin using a file and finishing off with sand-paper. After filing, ensure that the surfaces are parallel and that the angles are consistent. The remaining details, such as the supports, were made from strips of plastic and pieces of copper wire.

The smoke grenade dis-chargers were made from plastic tube. Tube was also used

to make the lens hood for the main gun/launcher sight, situated on the right side of the weapon.

The main gun/launcher was entirely rebuilt. The execution of this process was simple; tin tubes with 5–8cm diameters were fitted into each other. The most complictated part was working where the tubes joined. In the end circles of plastic card were slipped over the tubes to make the join.

The hull was transformed by adding extra details. Beginning at the rear section where the engine ventilation grilles are, openings were covered using 0.2mm or 0.3mm plastic sheet and the hinges were also re-worked. The other ventilation grilles and handles were improved by making new ones using strips of plastic formed

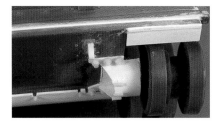

Reconstruction of the front wheel axle protector, made with plastic sheet, rivets and small rods.

Fuel intakes detailed with metal wire.

The lines of division of the hull have to be detailed.

The front wheel has a shock absorber, made of plastic tubing.

Resin headlights come from the M60 kit; the protector is made from with brass.

As well as the rivets, the hull has a small hole, which is made of 0.2mm thick sheet.

All the way around the hull is the flotation screen, erected when the Sheridan needed to wade (it was propelled in water by its tracks). This needs to be carefully modelled, because it does not lie perfectly flat on the surface of the hull and is held down by clamps. Each of these needs careful work and close reference to photographs of the vehicle in the field. Often these clamps were left open and can be modelled in this position. One important modification is to the rearmost clamp, which on the model appears vertical when it should be inclined and so form a right angle with the sloped rear plate. This is best eliminated and reconstructed with tin sheet, the best material from which to make the flotation screen clamps.

Lastly, you need to add the rivets along the sides: these can either be from with the designed Todo Modelismo etched-brass sheet by cutting and gluing or can be cutting from the thinnest Evergreen plastic rod with fine punch pliers; the edges then need softening with a Scotch Brite-type scouring pad or steel wool, after gluing in place.

accordingly, and copper wire for the handles. The inclined upper surfaces were reworked using fine strips of plastic, and the tool hooks and handles were made from a fine tin sheet, copper wire, and plastic sheets of varying thicknesses. The bottom photographs on pages 20–21 show the work done on the rear of the tank.

The front, on its lower part, needs reworking (see photograph above). The return wheel axle protectors, the mudflaps and the tow cable hooks are made from plastic sheet and rods, while the nuts are taken from the resin kit from Verlinden. The headlights are also made of this material (they belong to the previously mentioned M60 kit) their protectors are made from copper, with the addition of some small pieces of brass.

Painting

After World War II, the United States used the M41 Walker Bulldog tank and the self-propelled M56 gun as support for its airborne forces, but it was a temporary solution that did not cover their specialised requirements. In 1959 the profile appeared for the construction of the vehicle needed for this role, the requirements being a light, agile and powerful vehicle, with a great fire capacity. The Allison Division (of General Motors) was given responsibility for its development and quickly added numerous innovations to the specification while it was still on the drawing-board.

First the hull was to be of duralumin, and it was designed with welded air chambers on the sides. It was fitted with a flotation screen and a classic roller train with torsion bars without return rollers. For the turret, steel was used with very angled plates, and to avoid the problems of a wide barrel, the classic 90mm provided the basis for a new 152mm mixed barrel-missile launch system. As secondary armament, a coaxial 7.62mm machine gun was installed, with another, 12.7mm (0.5in), on the exterior. The engine was a 300hp diesel, and

the resulting final weight, 16 tons.

The vehicle appeared to be suitable — the parachute launch tests were spectacular and were carried out without difficulties — but later on, in service, the M551's performance was disappointing. In the end only

1,700 vehicles were built.

With the escalation of US forces' involvement in Vietnam, in spite of strong views against using tanks in the jungle, the M551 saw active service and proved to be a disappointment, given that its characteristics appeared adequate for such a

Washing with ochre (Vallejo 817) airbrush acrylic.

In the wet area, add small quantities of olive green (816).

Slight vertical touches blur the brush strokes.

The lighter marks are made with white (823), mixed with ochre (817) and a little umber (821).

By varying the quantities of colour, the different tones and shades are obtained.

On the rear the earthy tone is intensified by adding 823 white with 820 mahogany and 817 ochre brown.

The parts near the caterpillar tracks have an earthier tone, obtained with 814 umber, white and ochre.

An operational tank has very uneven paintwork, with discoloration produced by dust, mud, rain, etc.

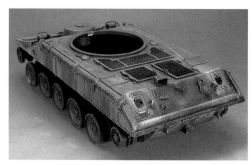

mixture of forest, river and marshy terrain. In fact, the limited protection of the light aluminium hull saw them quickly put out of combat. Individual crews began to introduce modifications, such as reinforcement of the lower glacis with additional armour plates, sandbags to reduce the threat of HESH and other stand-off weaponry.

Additionally the Sheridan was quite small internally — something that led to a field-modified carrier basket being added to carry ammunition for the light weapons, the crew's equipment as well as a large quantity of empty boxes of 20mm ammunition, which also served as a screen against hollow-charge projectiles. With these improvements the crew gained a measure of safety, which allowed a rapid evacuation of the vehicle before secondary explosions could take place. The M551 was most effective when it was used in cleaning up and

woodland pursuit operations, far from roads. Its lightness and fording capacity — helped by its flotation ability — made it ideal for penetrating forests and overcoming obstacles and terrain where the heavy M48 main battle tanks were easily bogged down. For some operations, a second 0.5in. weapon was added on the left side of the turret; it was operated from the peep-hole located there. The main gun was

used mainly with fragmentation ammunition, although the loading system was slower than in conventional weapons.

In spite of its shortcomings, the M551 Sheridan was used throughout the Vietnam conflict and, subsequently was on the inventory of the OPFOR units in war training at Fort Irwing, simulating Soviet vehicles.

When it seemed that its operational days were over, it again was put to service in the

'policing' actions that the USA performed on the island of Granada and in Panama, as well as being in the first contingent of armoured forces that arrived in the Gulf for Operation 'Desert Storm'.

The Scale Model

The Sheridan, which had previously passed largely unnoticed by model makers, in fact participated in many actions that transform it into an

On the wheels we use a wash of 821 umber. Later, with dry brush, golden brown a-86 and b-17 beige are applied.

The turret has a similar treatment, accentuating the effects of wear on the roof.

interesting vehicle. These were mainly in Vietnam, and the interest comes as a result of the many field modifications devised on the spot, both in terms of appliqué armour, equipment and of marking personalisations.

The only scale model available at 1/35 is manufactured by Academy Minicraft, an old mould by Tamiya, whose design can be improved considerably, as has already been shown.

Colour base using 821 umber and black for the rubber pads.

Touches of grey applied with a dry brush define the pads.

The final version: only the interior has a brown tone and a touch of black applied by dry brush.

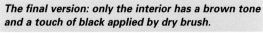

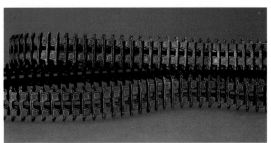

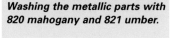

Washing the metallic parts with 820 mahogany and 821 umber.

B-17 beige is applied by dry brush to dust.

Painting and Camouflage

The basic colour of most of the American vehicles in Vietnam was dark olive green — but as well as this, one common element on all vehicles in the theatre was the dirtiness caused by the fine Vietnamese dust, normally reddish or yellow and very sticky. This is immediately apparent from the colour photos available of this war.

Generally, washes and dry brush techniques are used to bring out the shape of these single colour vehicles; however, although this usually does the trick, they don't look particularly realistic, and we want as much realism as possible, so that the scale model gives the impression of being an operational tank.

The figures of the crew are from a Verlinden resin kit.

The problem with the dirt is that if it is done without skill the results look ugly. Dust or dirt effects require a multiple treatment of base coats, washes, dry brush and airbrush work to look good. The main treatment is with paintbrush and acrylic.

As a first step, we covered the entire vehicle with dark olive (XF-62 from Tamiya) and for the general dust and dirt we use the following acrylic airbrush colours by Vallejo: burnt sienna

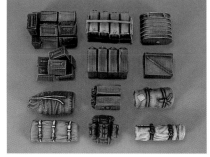

The numerous bits of additional equipment — ammunition boxes, rations, gas cans and tarpaulins — are also by Verlinden.

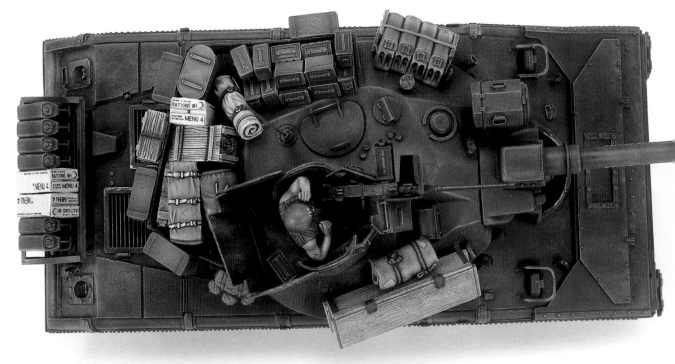

The base green is combined with ochre, brown and olive green to get different shades.

Mud made with 821 umber, a-86 golden brown and b-17 beige.

The lettering 'Pandora' is painted in red and white by hand.

The eye and the lettering "Cat Eye" are hand painted.

Microphones have been added to crew helmets.

The wooden box is first painted yellow, then washed with umber and finished with umber, beige and white using a dry brush.

The armour is decorated with slogans.

The resin equipment and accessories are manufactured by Verlinden.

blurred, without harsh lines. The proportions of the colours can be varied to obtain different tones, such as particularly on the front and rear of the vehicle, (where the dust and mud would build up) by adding a mahogany colour. After finishing the blended tones the dry brush process begins. For this we normally use paler shades taken from the same range as that used on the base, this is achieved by simply adding white to lighten the colour. The result is a weakening of the tone with a very marked contrast, for which it is necessary to use at least three lighter tones and to mix the base colour (dark olive) with

(321), golden brown (318), olive green (316), mahogany (320) and white (823).

The application is as follows: first a wash of very dilute golden brown is applied on the area to be painted. Before it dries, add small touches of burnt sienna and olive green with a brush; this work is distributed in fine lines from top to bottom, since, as it is applied onto a damp base, the colour expands without leaving hard lines.

Next, a base mixture is made with golden brown and a little burnt shade. This is applied onto small areas of the still damp paint, with a line that is sometimes vertical and occasionally small isolated splotches; the important thing is for the colour to be slightly

white and other colours, in this case yellow or even golden brown, to obtain good results. In the first tone there will be little difference, just enough so that it is barely noticeable. The colour tone will vary throughout, since in some places it will have more of a tendency towards one rather than the other colour, this is made by adding olive green plus a little burnt shade, since depending on the amount, the green becomes more or less brown. On the parts most affected by the dust and mud splattering, a second colour is applied with a white, golden brown and some natural shade. As a complementary touch, for a paler effect, white and golden brown are applied.

By the end of this treatment at

least five tones have been used, including the base colour — this same selection will be used for the whole model, but varying the proportion of the colours as necessary. As a penultimate touch, a wash is made with a mixture of olive green and burnt shade, trying to concentrate the colour in the grooves and removing the excess paint with the tip of a paintbrush. When all this dries the general outline of the shapes will be apparent. This process is completed with a soft dry brush, which only affects the rivets, angles and very clearly defined forms: for this we used green with paler greens, browns with beige or creams, and so on.

Roller Train and Tracks

Painting the rubber on the wheels is surprisingly hard work. The quickest procedure is to use quite a fluid colour, such as black (9324) acrylic by Vallejo, and then lighten it with slightly brownish grey, mainly to define the borders. The rest of the wheel is painted in a natural shade, lightening first with golden brown (a-36 from Film Color) or then with a mixture of white and natural shade. It is important to work the paintbrush in a circular motion, following the shape of the tyre. To finish, we applied a natural shade wash with a little olive green in the centre circle, then a soft beige touch with a dry

brush to bring out the shape of the nuts.

Although the tracks often present a problem, they are in fact quite easy to paint: in this case we find a mixed type with metal and rubber pads. The first step is to apply a coat of acrylic burnt shade with an airbrush; then, with black by Film Color, we paint all the pads. It is not necessary to do them one by one, they can be done with a continuous line, because they only stand out if the pads are marked and nothing else.

Next we prepare a mixture of mahogany and burnt umber, giving a wash with the colour as it comes out of the pot, covering the metallic parts. Allow this to dry completely before finishing with a beige application with a dry brush — although a metallic grey can also be used, depending on the terrain where the vehicle is positioned.

The ammunition boxes and petrol drums have the same general colour as the tank, but vary it by adding a little black to the white, also green and yellow

when the light green tone is prepared before applying the dry brush.

The wooden boxes are painted yellow and a wash of natural shade, using a dry brush for beige and a little yellow.

The most characteristic element of these vehicles was the prolific lettering and mascots painted all over the tank — these slogans can be used, also characters from cartoons, comics or TV — always keeping in mind that they have to be contemporary for 1972.

M60A1 RISE

Until recently, the M60A1 was the US Marine Corps' main battle tank; it has now been replaced by the modern M1A1 Abrams.

Until the arrival of the M1A1, the USMC was forced to modernise its already obsolete M60s and to face a period of transition. The corps decided to make its own a project that the US Army had previously rejected, inspired by the 'Blazer' reactive armour developed by the Israelis. The successes obtained by the Israeli army with reactive armour prompted the US Army to make its own version of this, known as 'Rise'.

Reactive armour consists of a series of boxes or blocks placed on the surfaces of the vehicle, each of which contains a small explosive charge, that detonates when hit by a projectile of a suitable size. By exploding it prevents the projectile penetrating the tank. Small calibre ammunition does not set off this reactive armour.

In contrast to the Israeli Blazer, and as an added measure to protect against penetration, the Rise system is not flush with

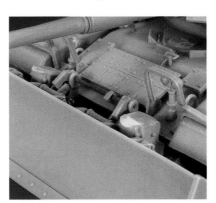

The M9 dozer blade is resin and comes from Verlinden. It is necessary to detail various elements of its anchoring and operating system, and also to modify some details of the front part of the upper hull.

The model looks better with wheels from the Tamiya kit.

The pipes of the dozer blade's hydraulic system stand out on the rear part of the upper hull.

the turret armour. The new M60A1, equipped with this armour, entered service in 1988.

The Scale Model

At the moment there are a large variety of M60 kits on the market, reproducing all its variants. At 1/35 scale Tamiya brand has the M60A3 and M60A1 Rise variants in its catalogue, while Academy-Minicraft markets two scale models of the M60A1 with reactive armour, both the American Rise and the Israeli Blazer, with the latter including the KTM-4 mineroller. Finally,

Esci has among its products the M60A1, M60A3 and M60A1 Blazer.

Traditionally, Esci has been well known for its model tanks and military vehicles at 1/72

The commander's cupola comes from the Academy kit.

Etched brass is used to modify various elements, particularly to the supports and reinforcements.

First we eliminated the left skirting and the plate to support the rear box, so we can install the fuel tank for the blade's hydraulic gear. To detail the tank, we used the Verlinden kit, mounting the angle irons that support the reactive armour boxes, the air filters and the stowage boxes for the smoke grenades. We also added the protective sleeve for the hydraulic system pipes that work the dozer blade, and the box that houses the telephone for communications with the tank crew.

The cage or basket at the rear of the turret is a delicate assembly which is best added after the rest of the accessories and equipment.

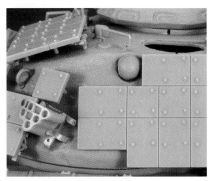

Carefully check the correct location of the reactive armour boxes before, drilling their retaining holes.

The position of the plates on the front part of the turret and the hull is quite haphazard.

scale, but it is appropriate to point out that the company's M60 1/35 is a splendid piece of work with a remarkable level of detailing.

Assembly

As a base for this model, we used the Esci M60A3, but we could also have used the M60A1 from the same brand. To reproduce the Rise version, we cannibalised the Tamiya kit, from which we took the reactive armour boxes and road wheels as key elements. The blade is a Verlinden resin accessory.

First the suspension units were mounted. Next the blade was assembled, along with the detail of its hydraulic systems.

Then we assembled the upper hull — the area of the model that has had the most modification.

On the front we moved the headlights and their guards to the correct position (check against photographs or scale drawings to get this right). Finally, we mounted the other bits of the dozer blade's hydraulic system.

To assemble the turret, we first glued the two parts that make it up and then added the pediment. The rear basket and the barrel came from the Tamiya kit, as did the protector for the gunner's periscope, because Esci does not reproduce the one that belongs to the M60A1 version. Also from the Tamiya kit came parts of the commander's machine gun and the hand rails located next to the loader's hatch, as these are only present in the M60A1 Rise configuration.

Once we had placed the hand rails and laser targeting system sensors on the turret sides, we went on to mount the smoke launchers.

The commander's cupola

The Verlinden figures have been slightly modified.

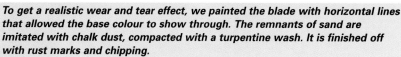

To get a realistic wear and tear effect, we painted the blade with horizontal lines that allowed the base colour to show through. The remnants of sand are imitated with chalk dust, compacted with a turpentine wash. It is finished off with rust marks and chipping.

The armour plates have been painted with a slightly different tone to that used to paint the tank's overall camouflage.

came from the Academy model, as it is the one with the most detail. However, the actual hatch — and that of the loader — are from the Tamiya model, because it is easier to detail these with etched-brass accessories.

Finally, we worked on the reactive armour boxes and then drilled the appropriate holes to fix them on the hull and the turret.

Painting

Our scale model represents a M60A1 Rise equipped with an M9 blade, as used in a training exercise at 29 Palms — the US Marine base in California's Mojave desert. The tank is from to the 1st Battalion of the 7th MEB (Marine Expeditionary Brigade), a unit specially trained for combat in desert conditions. These tanks have a number of tactical markings — white 'V's placed in various positions, indicating to which company they belong, and white bands at the tip of the barrel to indicate the platoon to which the vehicle is assigned; these bands are usually also painted on the rear left mud flap.

Weathering and ageing the model is not easy. The M60s of the USMC (and also of the US Army) have operated in all climatic conditions and geographic locations, from the heat and dust of the desert to the cold and damp of the

European fields and forests. On top of this, we had to add the effects caused by the crew moving about on and using the tank. Then, because of frequent cleaning with high pressure hoses every time an exercise is concluded, rust marks and peeling paintwork appear exposing the base green layer with which the tanks were originally painted in the Chrysler factories in the 1970s, and the chipped paintwork reveals the base metal. All this is without counting the legacy of dirt and damage characteristic of each operational environment!

Base Paint

The base colour was made with forest green (150) and matt sand (63, both enamels from Humbrol). To try to vary the sand colour tone towards a predominantly greyish khaki finish, but without losing the vivacity of the original tone, we applied a thin, quite dilute coat of a mixture of matt earth (XF-52) and khaki (XF-49, in this case from Tamiya). To finish reproducing the camouflage, the black and whitish marks were added — these are not actually white, but rather a very pale khaki tone, achieved using Vallejo acrylics.

The reactive armour plates were painted separately from the rest of the scale model, applying pale green (117 from

Humbrol), somewhat darker than the green of the camouflage, since in the reference photos this difference is appreciable. The 'V' at the front was reproduced in acrylic white by airbrush using masking. The bands on the barrel were done in the same way.

We finished this phase by applying by airbrush a coat of Tamiya acrylic gloss varnish, dissolved in plenty of water; this gives a glossy finish that enhances the forms and colours of the model.

Ageing

Initially, and to blend the colours composing the camouflage, we applied a general oil wash with natural sienna earth and burnt earth shades. On the tank's hull, as well as the two washes already mentioned, we added another wash of yellow ochre, to intensify the effect of the dust and accumulated dirt.

Once these colours were dry, the details — such as bolts and grooves — were emphasised, also with washes, but in this case selectively and in a shade of black, both in enamels and oil. It is important to dampen the area on which the black is applied with plenty of paint thinner or solvent, so that the paint blends well and rims or unsightly contours do not appear. It is a good idea to limit

The effect of choppy paintwork is clearer on the parts most affected by impacts and friction, and also on the large surfaces and the turret.

To imitate the dust on the tank, we applied a layer of colour with an airbrush, particularly over the curved and horizontal surfaces.

yourself to a small area, so as to have time to bring out all the detail before the paint dries and the paint thinner evaporates. This technique is also used to imitate the grease accumulated around nuts, etc.

After doing this, we went on to reproduce different ageing and wearing effects, such as chips and holes, repairs or stains left by spilled fuel. This is a delicate operation; to get it right means some research — best carried out at a museum or military open day — on how painted armour surfaces age over time

The effect of choppy painting was achieved with the colour olive drab (XF-62 from Tamiya), applied as with the sand stains and made paler with khaki on the greens. Using a very fine paintbrush, we painted tiny marks, with the smallest amount of paint possible.

The chips on the metal were imitated most on the green stains, since it is there that they are most noticeable in the photos of these tanks; the same pictures show that they are more localised and less numerous on the areas painted

The chips on the metal are reproduced in the same way as the choppy paintwork was done, going over the edges particularly.

When painting the tracks, we apply a black base slightly tinged with brown and on this an initial sand coloured wash and then hide colour, mixing with burnt sienna oil.

in sand colour. The process was same as before, but in this case the colours were a mixture of metallic grey (XF-56) and olive drab (XF-62), making the metal stains more in harmony with the colour of their environment and ensuring that they did not stand out excessively.

The rust marks were made with a burnt sienna oil base and intensified in the central area with the colour leather (62 from Humbrol), imitating a rusted and aged appearance. Around the fuel intakes, some stains were made by means of a mixture of burnt earth and dark cobalt blue

oils. The bluish tone this makes imitates quite realistically the effect of gasoline spilled while filling the tank.

Accessories

Most of the accessories are the usual kind found on any modern US tank, but the box hanging on the right side and the two tarpaulin covers on the left are very characteristic of the personal equipment of the M6OA1 Rise. The figures belong to the Israeli tank crew (cold-wet dress) by Verlinden Productions (ref. no. 529), and they have

To paint the huge quantity of equipment and accessories realistically, use the largest possible variety of tonal variations from one element to the next.

The white marking was painted with an airbrush and mask.

Elements Used

– M6OA3, ESCI ref. 5040
– M60A3 Rise TAMIYA ref. 35157
– M48/M60 Update set. VERLINDEN ref. 320
– M60A3 Dozer Blade, VER-LINDEN ref. 499

Bibliography

M60 Patton in Action, Squadron Signal Publications.
M60A3. War Machines no. 3. Verlinden Publications.
On the Road to Kuwait, Marines in the Gulf, War Machines no. 13, Verlinden Publications.
M60, Concord.
USMC firepower, Armor & Artillery, Concord.
Sword in the Sand, U.S. Marines in the Gulf War, Concord.
Ejércitos de tierra en la Guerra del Golfo, Osprey Military.

been modified by replacing the original heads with others included in Desert Storm tank/APC crew by the same manufacturer (ref. no. 596). The intercom system was detailed with fine copper wire.

Israeli M60

In spite of the combination of painting techniques, conversion kits and superdetailing, it is still difficult at times to make your models stand out from the crowd. One way to do this is to concentrate on the tank crew themselves, the figures, uniforms and incidental, personal equipment. Do this by adapting different kits and by using models made from different materials — such as using resins modified by heating.

The Scale Model

This is the Tamiya 1/35 scale model of an Israeli M60 used in the Lebanon in 1982-83. One of the most appealing facets of this model is the Blazer reactive armour and the comparison it affords with the M60A1 Rise in the last section. We also used the Verlinden Israeli M60 conversion kit plus some ammunition boxes also by Verlinden.

The equipment is arranged in such a way that the heavy elements — boxes, containers, etc — are at the bottom, and the knapsacks, mattresses, etc are piled on top.

The figures were remodelled, the details of the uniform eliminated with a knife and the new ones added with putty.

An important detail is that all the packages are perfectly secured with straps or ropes.

Assembly and Detailing

In addition to the basic model and Verlinden accessories other materials needed to build the model included epoxy putty, copper wire of different sizes, tin strips, plastic sheets and some bits and pieces from other kits.

Assembly was straightforward: however, when converting or modifying a model it is important to ensure that you do not include any pieces that should be excluded in the conversion such as machine gun mountings, headlight protection, anchorage for antennas, etc. Check the reference photos carefully!

The faces of the crew were slightly modified, with the beards added.

The basic vehicle used is the Tamiya M60, with a Verlinden conversion kit.

The bundles fit perfectly, bulging to give with the impression of weight and shapes fitting together.

The mattresses have natural creases; they are made when the putty is still soft.

The resin elements, as usual, must be filed and smoothed to eliminate excess bits. Some the fixings for the reactive armour boxes on the front of the turret had to be modified.

The protectors for the headlights were made from scratch with fine plastic sheet and wire mesh; we also used this material for the strap grips and ropes for the equipment.

The machine gun mounting is superdetailed with pieces of plastic and rods; the antennas were made of stretched plastic and metal wire. The rubber track pads were worn down; this effect is achieved by cutting with a knife and slightly burning the pads with a hot tip.

Modelling the Equipment

The additional equipment is made up of elements from various kits, Verlinden ammunition boxes, food, etc, and other spare pieces; they generally need to be detailed by adding ropes, wires and so on.

The most unrealistic thing about these accessories is their rigidity; they just don't sit well together, they don't have the size or weight to mould themselves together as happens in real life. To avoid this, we have to combine the plastic or moulded pieces of kits with other scrtach-built pieces that we make for ourselves out of epoxy plastic putty so that we can imitate the sag of, sacks, tarpaulins and mattresses. As these are being modelled, and while they are still soft, they are adapted, curved and shaped realistically to avoid the rigidity of the plastic and the resin kits. Any of the many putties

To achieve a lifelike appearance for these elements, specific publications are consulted, specifically Battleground Lebanon published by Concord.

available can be used. These can be bought in hardware stores and modelling shops. The shapes can be copied from photos or the kits themselves. Modelling naval ropes and tin sheet can be used for the straps to complete the pieces. Remember that everything must be bundled up and secured.

Transforming Figures

The crew member enclosed with the kit was used as the officer on the tank by filing and sanding his helmet to adapt him to his new function. The uniform also had to be changed to turn him into an Israeli tank soldier. All unsuitable details were eliminated with a knife and replaced with the correct ones made from modelling putty, applied in small quantities, to form pockets, zips, seams, etc. The beards were also modelled with putty. The other crew member is put together with a mixture of different bodies and arms, and a head from the kit by Verlinden; the uniform is also remodelled with putty.

Study action photos to decide what equipment can be added.

Use putty for curved shapes and resin or plastic for angles.

Howitzer Motor Carriage M43

While main battle tanks and armoured cars are the most obvious form of armour modelled, mobile artillery makes a good alternative, often marrying interesting detailing techniques with a full guncrew.

The origin of the M43 is closely linked to that of the M40, with the creation in 1943 of the so-called Medium Weight Combat Team, in which the designs of the T83 (M40) and T89 (M43) were included. Basically the two models had the same components and configuration, and the only difference between them was the type of gun used and the layout of the firing area. Although the construction of 576 T89s was ordered, only 48 had

been built by the end of the war, with 24 of these being M40 conversions. The main difference between the two was that the M40 stowed its 155mm rounds in ammunition containers around the firing area. These were removed on the M43 as the ammunition for the 203mm gun was stored in a vehicle that was specially designed for it. This had the added advantage of significantly increasing the guncrew's working space.

In January 1945, a T83 (M43) and a T89 (M40) were sent to the European Theatre to be evaluated. In February 1945 they took part in Operation 'Zebra'. The T89 was assigned to the 991st Campaign Artillery Battalion alongside the T83 and M12.

The M43 was used effectively in the Korean War, mainly to carry out counter-battery fire, and was undoubtedly the weapon most feared by the communists.

Components

Long Tom by Azimut.
M3A3 by Tamiya (no. 122).
Roller Train HVSS by MP Model.
Both the resin kit by Verlinden, (ref. no 845) and the injected plastic one marketed by AFV can also be used.
Rods and plastic sheets by Evergreen.
Silicone and resin.
Products necessary to carry out etched-brass detailing.

The Scale Model

To make this M43, we started by copying in resin all the parts that this vehicle had in common with the M40. Although as a base reference we used the colour photo that appears in the book *Armor in Korea*, it was of great help to find another photo of the same vehicle in the book *Modern American Armor*, since from this one could clearly

appreciate that the M43 is a modified M40. This means that the interior must have the large chests from the M40 and not the distribution of the projectiles and 8in charges that appear in the technical manual.

As a basis for the construction of the hull, engine chamber, combat chamber, driver's chamber, chests, support base for the cannon, mud flaps, roller train, platforms and grid, we used an M40, although there are some slight differences between the two models, which we will clarify below.

Ammunition Storage

As the M43 is so similar to the M40, the distribution of the ammunition storage has followed a parallel path, but with three different configurations (see drawings at the bottom of page 43:

A — Layout of the initial prototype, shared by T89 and T83, in which the containers could house both the 155mm and the 203mm ammunition.
B — Layout of the M43s modified from M40s, in which the 155mm containers were

M43 TECHNICAL CHARACTERISTICS

Length: 6.65m
Height: 2.84m
Width: 3.14m
Weight: 37.195kg
Armour: 12–100mm
Crew: 8
Propulsion unit: Continental 9-cylinder, radial R975-C4
Armament: An 8in (293mm) howitzer 6-shot M1
Maximum speed: 38km/h
Range: 160km
Manufacturer: Pressed Steel Car Co. Pittsburgh, Pa.

eliminated, leaving extra crew space. The projectiles and charges were transported in another vehicle.
C — This configuration had eight complete projectiles and charges on either side.

On the market currently are two different types of 203mm ammunition (one marketed by Verlinden and the other an injected plastic scale model of the TOA M548 ammunition from AFV); the following is only given as a guide for those who want to build this particular model.

Gun

The gun used for the construction of the vehicle is the Long Tom marketed by Azimut in its 8in. version, although at the moment we have two other models available on the market, one in resin from Verlinden and another in injected plastic from AFV. In this section we will describe the modifications to make to the Azimut kit:

– Detail the guides
– Detail the screwed sections

General rear view, where the blade and its operating system stand out. Some pieces have been textured with putty to get a realistic finish when combined with the paintwork.

inside the closing block, if it is to be left open
– Detail the firing mechanism — the hammer and firing key
– Lower the bottom front part of the gun carriage by 3mm so that the unit has the correct height
– Add the clutch pedal for the gun
– Add the shield for the gun and its supports
– Add to the shield the box for the gunner's quadrant
– Complete all the supports and viewfinders, both direct and indirect
– Make the immobilisation supports for the barrel during movement

Painting

Following the standard for American vehicles of the time, for the painting of the M43 we have used olive drab (XF-62) from Tamiya. This is toned down with a little yellow, using the usual techniques age the vehicle, namely dry brush, blending with oil, chalks and inks.

Shown in this photo is the diversity of materials used in the construction of the tank; these are mainly pieces copied in resin, combined with etched brass pieces, plus elements made with rods and plastic strips, etc.

View of the support to fasten the gun.

General detail of the gun, highly improved and super-detailed. Among other details, all the supports and viewfinders have been completely built from scratch.

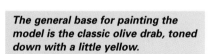

The general base for painting the model is the classic olive drab, toned down with a little yellow.

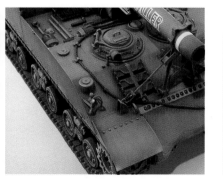

On some edges there appear the typical effects of chipped paintwork — these are made with touches of colour.

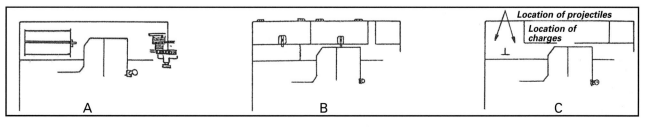

Location of projectiles

Location of charges

A   B   C

Markings

Both for the yellow band and for the name 'The Killer', adhesive masking tape was used. See the stencil for each of the sides of the barrel.

Transfers from Decadry have been used for the letters USA and the number 40194822.

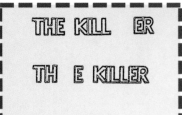

Bibliography

The Illustrated Encyclopedia of Military Vehicles, Ian V. Hogg and John Weeks, Hamlyn.

British and American Tanks, Peter Chamberlain and Chris Ellis, Arms & Armour.

Armor in Korea, Jim Mesko, Squadron Signal Publications Inc.

Armour of the Korean War 1950-53, Simon Dunstan, Osprey Vanguard, no. 27.

HMC M43 Technical Manual, Armor Research Company.

M40 Photo Set, Armor Research Company.

Máquinas de guerra, Peter Young, Grijalbo.

M4 Sherman, George Forty, Weapons and Warfare, Blandford prtess.

Modern American Armor, S. Zaloga & Loop. Arms & Armour Press.

Empleo táctico del armamenta, Fernando de Salas López.

Sherman, R.P. Hunnicutt.

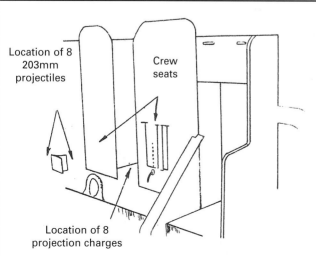

Location of 8 203mm projectiles

Crew seats

Location of 8 projection charges

To paint the lettering on the barrel, two masks were used — one for each colour.

Some effects of wear and tear are obtained using reddish brown tones, accentuating, in this case, the wear on the blade.

HOWITZER MOTOR CARRIAGE M41

The M41 is part of a large family of self-propelled vehicles, mostly American and mostly forgotten by the makers of scale models; this does not mean they are any less attractive to enthusiasts.

M19, M37, M40, and — as seen in the last section — M43, all vehicles that deserve a place in the field of model making. We hope that one day in the not too distant future a company will surprise us and decide to market them.

History

The self-propelled M41 gun has its origin in a project carried out on the chassis of the M5A1 Stuart. Two prototypes of this vehicle were built, the T16 (mounting a 4.5in cannon) and the T-64 (mounting a 155mm howitzer).

Before the introduction by the American army of the concept of 'Light Combat Equipment', both

Although the M-24 by Italeri is used as the basis, the upper part needs to be removed, using the hatches and the front part without the machine gun. The rest is reconstructed with plastic sheet.

The use of plastic sheet, strips and rods by Evergreen is fundamental for building the whole structure of the vehicle and the combat platform.

vehicles were revised and it was decided to replace the chassis of the M5A1 with that of the M24. The result was a vehicle similar in appearance to the M19, but mounting a 40mm anti-aircraft howitzer.

The versions following were denominated T16E1 and T64E1, although the first was quickly rejected even before the prototype was completed. The prototype for the T64E1 was tested in 1945, and the Massey-Harris company signed a contract to build 250, with the name self-propelled M41 gun (HMC). In fact only 60 of them participated in the Korean War.

The variations with respect to the original vehicle (M24) were significant, since, although the driver's compartment remained unchanged, the engine and the rest of the components were located behind the driver's chamber.

The howitzer model installed on the M41 was the 155M1 (transformed from the towed

Italeri 155mm howitzer; the top carriage needs to be lowered by 3 mm.

Combat chamber with the compartments for ammunition and their locks.

Front reconstructed with the elimination of the machine gun and the addition of a support fixture for the gun.

The grids are reconstructed with 0.20 x 0.40mm plastic strips.

version), and it was necessary to modify some aspects for it to be installed. Its mounting allowed the piece to cover a firing arc of 20.5° to the right and 17° to the left, with a possible range of 15km, thanks to its 45° of elevation.

Located in the rear is a dozer blade designed both to absorb recoil and, at the same time, to be used as support for a platform that extended the combat chamber, allowing the

crew to have extra space to work. Placed inside the combat chamber were housings to take the crew's personal armament, as well as for 22 155mm rounds.

Initially there was thought to be a need to build a vehicle to accompany the M41 to transport its ammunition; this project was cancelled in 1944, and instead both the M39 and armed trailers were used. Once it was completed, the M41 was handed over to the self-propelled units of the post-war army.

Nicknamed the 'Gorilla', the M41 entered combat in 1950 in the Korean War, and performed outstandingly, thanks to its mobility and size. Smaller than most other US mobile artillery, it could accompany infantry when they needed fire support. It was also used as conventional artillery from camouflaged positions, being able to change position quickly if discovered.

As a self-propelled piece of artillery the M41 performed well, but it is still not a very well known vehicle and the documentation available is surprisingly scarce.

The M41 had only a short service life, until later into the 1950s, and was withdrawn in the same decade it entered service.

Components

For the basis of this model we used the Italeri M24 Chaffee (no 244). We took mainly the front part (including the driver's cabin) and the running train. The Howitzer 155 M1A2 also came from Italeri (no 232), but we only used the tube and gun carriage, though they needed modifications to the direction and elevation system.

This vehicle ended up using both model T72E1 (initially) and then T85E1 (later) tracks, and we found that we preferred the former, as the model T72E1 was the more widely used. It must also be taken into account that the M41 is almost 1.5cm longer than the M24, so that the tracks in the Italeri kit are a touch short for this conversion; therefore it was necessary to cannibalise a piece from another model to get the extra length. In this case, we found it best to use the tracks provided by Accurate Armor. You will, however, be very surprised to find six sections of complete track in the pack (it does not have any loose link), which will give more than a few problems when coming to put them on the tractor and tensor wheels! The solution is to detail a link, make a mould, and make all the copies needed in resin. It is, in short, an expensive and irritating litle problem.

We also had to use 0.5mm and 1mm plastic card to make most of the pieces — it's a great help to have a stock of the wide range of plasticard sheets and rods available on the market. The ones used here were all from Evergreen.

You can tell from all this that construction of this vehicle was not at all cheap, but the satisfaction that it gave made it all worthwhile. Because of this, and because of the amount of scratch-building needed, you must make sure you have a very clear idea of the vehicle you intend to build and work out exactly what you'll need to build it. Most important is the reference material — as already mentioned — good photo references and detailed scale drawings so that you can build suitable templates. Unfortunately, we do not have room to provide these in this book: you must research them from publications on the market or buy them.

In spite of the cost, it is very instructive to take on this type of construction for the lessons that can be learned.

Construction

Before beginning to assemble the model, keep in mind the scale. It can be distorted very easily — particularly when joining the parts together if you don't take the thickness of the plastic card into account.

We divided the construction into separate sections:

Lower hull
From the scale model of the M24 we cut away with a saw bottom of the model, retaining the top part (including the back steps) and the upper hull including the

The front armour plating must be centred, as the machine gun has been removed.

support arms of the road wheels. We replaced the lower hull with plastic card cut to size from scale drawings and with all joins reinforced. Keep in mind that it is much more convenient to reinforce all the joins at this stage rather than leaving it to later.

Upper hull
Work on the separated upper hull was extensive and involved eliminating the hull machine gun and building a framework onto which we could build from plastic card hatches, engine grilles, fuel intakes and other details. Relevant pieces of the M24 model were used wherever possible. The engine grid was built from 0.20 x 0.40mm plastic card, available from Evergreen.

Once these operations have been done, we placed the upper onto our scratch-built lower hull and then added the track guards. Next we started on the firing platform.

Main hatch platform, the ground relief is made with wire previously shaped into the characteristic design.
The rear blade is fully reconstructed with plastic strip and sheet.

Firing platform

The firing platform is in two pieces, the compartment itself, which is built up from plastic card and fitted into the space left in the lower hull, and the stepped platform and dozer blade underneath.

We cut the floor from 1mm plastic card, detailed it with wire mesh stuck with cyanoacrylate, then with putty. The back end of the compartment was detailed to include ammunition racking, etc. The dozer blade was formed from 0.5mm plastic card, and shaped using heat to make the plastic malleable.

The Running Train

Construction of the tracks has already been mentioned. The road wheel assembly utilises parts from the M24 kit.

155mm howitzer

This was built following the instructions from the box, with one exception — the gun carriage was lowered by 3mm so that it was at the right height.

After completing these stages the model is ready for painting.

Painting

The colour used to complete the tank is the usual one for American vehicles from this era. We can use either olive drab from Humbrol (nos. 155 and 66, ref. HM3) or Tamiya (XF-62). However, the latter needs to have some yellow mixed in, because the original colour is quite dark.

For the finish on the metalled pieces, we used the colour magnesium from Testors. Remember, though, that this type of paint has to be used with an airbrush. To achieve a perfect finish, allow it to dry for a few minutes and then burnish it with a soft suede cloth to avoid scratching the paint.

T-62 BDD AFGHANISTAN

Sometimes the model maker finds himself attracted by vehicles for which there is frustratingly little graphic documentation. This means all too often that the project has to be abandoned, or at least postponed until more information is obtained.

Luckily this was not quite the case with our T-62 BDD, as we were able to find a single photo reference, published in Concord's *Armor of the Afghanistan War*. We had to use other sources when it came to detailing the tank.

Our T-62 is from the latest generation and therefore incorporates technical advances such as the thermal sleeve for the gun (that used on the T-72), a KTD2 laser rangefinder, the cupola modified to mount a Dshk Duskha, and finally the spectacular BDD appliqué armour at the front, on both sides of the turret, and another anti-mine piece located on the lower front area of the tank.

To this point everything is the same as the other T-62 BDDs of the 1980s, but what makes this one unique is the arrangement of welded grids on the sides of the turret and chassis, which serve as protection against

Plasticard has been extensively used, particularly on the glacis appliqué armour because of the poor quality of the pieces supplied in the MB kit, which served solely as a guide for the correct measurements.

To detail the turret, various accessories from Tamiya and Verlinden were used, complemented with etched-brass pieces

The grids welded to the turret are reproduced using fine copper wire to build up a mesh.

Rear view. Showing the plasticard fixings for the drums and etched-brass ventilation grids.

Some breakage or distortion of the grids give greater realism to the finished model.

The side protection grids are composed of plasticard segments and fine longitudinal strips or rods of copper.

To be able to leave the side box lid open, it is necessary to reduce its thickness with a milling machine. The exhaust pipe is etched brass.

RPGs and replace the classic side skirts that these tanks normally sported. These grids were probably hastily welded onto the tank while it was in the battlefield. The job would have been improvised, with the appliqué armour obtained from a destroyed industrial area or 'liberated' from a handy shed, in much the same way as their predecessors had modified their vehicles in World War II. When the Soviets entered Berlin, they welded similar armour onto their T-34/85s.

As regards camouflage, we ignored the dark green shown in the photo, preferring to reproduce the striped sand brown and green design with which the T-62s was usually camouflaged.

The wording on the turret occupies the whole side plate and probably refers to some heroic act. Finally, we must point out that our model does not include the mudguards, since these were usually lost in combat or were dismantled by the crew, as they tended to bend inwards and become twisted by the tracks.

How the T-62 BDD looks once the assembly phase is completed — the additions and modifications make all the difference.

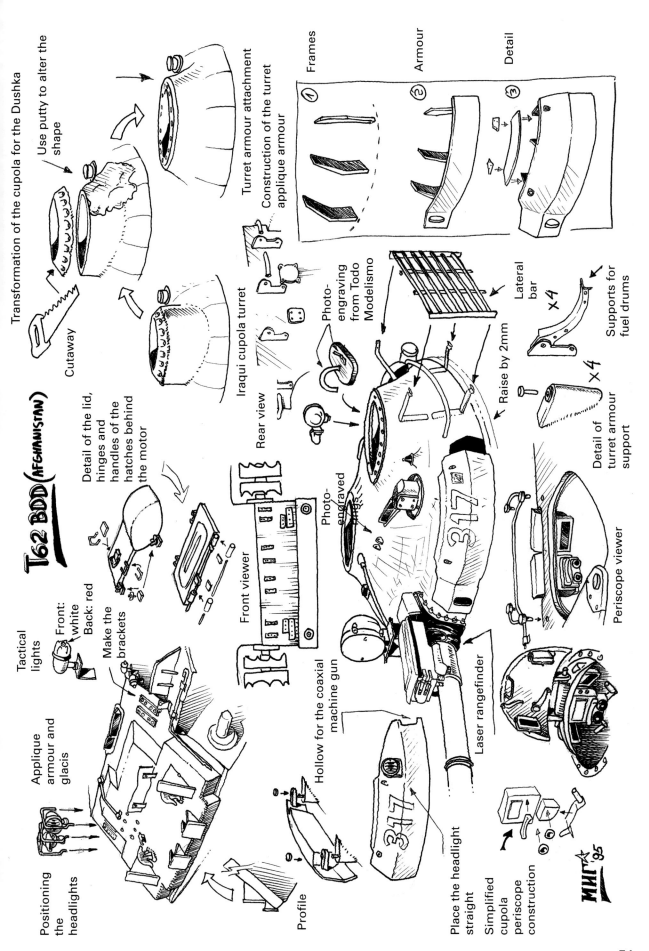

Transformation of the cupola for the Dushka

Use putty to alter the shape

Cutaway

Frames

Armour

Detail

Turret armour attachment

Construction of the turret applique armour

Iraqui cupola turret

Rear view

Photo-engraving from Todo Modelismo

Lateral bar
×4

×4

Detail of turret armour support

Supports for fuel drums

Periscope viewer

T62 BDD (AFGHANISTAN)

Detail of the lid, hinges and handles of the hatches behind the motor

Tactical lights

Front: white
Back: red

Make the brackets

Front viewer

Photo-engraved

Raise by 2mm

Applique armour and glacis

Positioning the headlights

Hollow for the coaxial machine gun

Profile

Place the headlight straight

Simplified cupola periscope construction

Laser rangefinder

МИГ '95

51

Assembly

To do this, we started from the Tamiya scale model and then modified it and detailed it to be as close as possible to the latest generation T-62 BDD.

To reproduce the BDD armour we started with the MB resin kit, but only to take the measurements, as we had to reconstruct them in their entirety due to the poor quality of the kit in question. The curved pieces that go round the outside of the turret were the most difficult to produce, because they had to be made from plastic card. We carefully took the measurements of the original and used a variety of photos for support. The new pieces were built like ships in a shipyard, using reinforcing ribs and later covering them with plastic sheets. In any event, it was very tricky to get the slight curvatures, which is why we advise you not to attempt this frustrating enterprise if you have enough money to buy the kit

As well as building the front armour, the forward part of the tank is heavily detailed by both scratch-built and proprietory items.

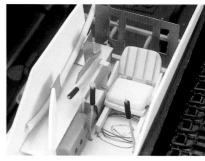

We have also reconstructed the interior of the driver's area, mostly made up with elements made of plasticard.

rather poor, so we used the resin turret offered by AEF Designs in its Iraqi T-62 conversion kit. This involved extra work, because I had to reconstruct the dome of the Duskha with VP putty and to remove the two supports for the hatch, so I could later add those from the Tamiya kit, which are better made. The TPN-1 viewfinder is also by Tamiya, as

well as the snorkel, the rear cover of the cases and all the ammunition. Finally, we had to raise the height of the turret by 2mm, as it is excessively low; we also sanded the surface of this a little to get rid of the excess texture. For the details of the vehicle, we used excellent etched-brass pieces from Eduard as they are remarkably

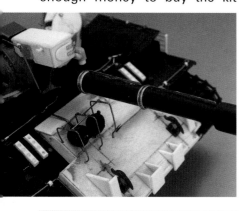

The thermal sleeve for the main gun is imitated with fine strips of aluminium and copper wire. The laser rangefinder is also scratch-built.

from DML. The photographs that accompany this section show clearly the details of the appliqué armour. After reconstructing the armour on the turret and the front, no further use was made of the MB kit.

We did not use the Tamiya turret because we found it slightly out of proportion and

they often appear in the photos, but I had to reduce them with the milling machine to get a realistic depth.

The laser rangefinder does not offer much difficulty after making the armour for the turret, but the problem is that it does not come in the MB kit and it needs to be reconstructed from photographs. The barrel has a thermal cover, which is imitated with aluminium strips and copper wire. The end of the barrel needs to be narrowed, because the Tamiya one is rather thick. The side drums are detailed with copper wire and pieces of motorbike cable to simulate the pipes.

The interior is made up from pieces of various origin and plastic card, with the sole purpose that the spectator does not see an empty space. It is not necessary to reproduce the interior to the letter, since this would only waste time and the work involved would not be appreciated.

Painting

For many people this is the most important and enjoyable phase in model making. For this very reason, we should not lapse into routine application and end up painting all tanks the same way. Each tank and vehicle is different, and each should be painted in a different way. It is wrong to think that two tanks from different periods or settings can be painted the same way. Of course, each modeller has his own recognisable style, but we must take a few risks when painting a model and attempt to adapt our knowledge and discoveries to each scale model we make.

The painting of this T-62 is a little atypical, not because of the final result but the work on it in itself: 75 percent of the painting is filter-treated and washed, without using a dry brush. Furthermore, despite the tank's

The camouflage is composed of dark green (XF-61) and suede (XF-57), the latter lightened with white.

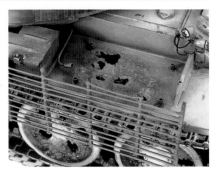

The lettering on the turret is done by hand with a brush, following the shape and size that can be seen on the photo of the actual vehicle.

economical as well as useful. However, in some areas, we also used pieces of etch-brass from Todo Modelismo.

Housed in the front lower section are the supports for the KMT-4 minesweepers — we used those from the Verlinden kit to detail the T-55. We made the anti-mine armour plate with plastic card, as well as the supports for the auxiliary fuel drums at the rear; these were finished with pieces of etched brass from the T-55. The boxes on the sides were left open as

The rust colour is applied with an airbrush to highlight the panels; washes bring out the reliefs, grooves and small details.

To reproduce the chipped paintwork effects, we used dark green XF-61 as the base.

The mud sticking to the wheels is imitated with a mixture of putty and sand, decorated later with different colour shades.

apparent chromatic richness, we only used four colours, with the exception, of course, of the colours for the component parts: figures, arms and mud. To find a reference for the correct paint job, I had to look for photos. In Afghanistan, vehicles with this camouflage did not become excessively discoloured as they did in desert conditions, but rather became extremely dusty and rusty, due to the winter climate there. The main work in the painting of this vehicle does not lie in the base colours, but the work on the dust effects and wear and tear.

Base colour

As already mentioned, the base is not the important thing, so we painted the whole tank green (XF-61) and later applied the striped camouflage with buff (XF-57) and white from Vallejo in a very irregular manner, applying most white onto the horizontal areas.

To paint the lateral grids we used different colours to those used to cover the rest of the tank.

Rust

For the rust, we used a mixture of Humbrol colours as a base, and then later applied the same with an airbrush. We used the same colour again for the washes. Before the washes we added a glaze, tinted slightly with the rust colour, which only changes the luminosity value of the base colour if it is used with turpentine and paint thinner, to give a totally glazed finish. The wash, loaded only with paint and paint thinner, brings out the grooves and rivets, giving relief to the scale model.

Dust effect

Continue with the four colours applied earlier; to do the chips in the paintwork, we used base colour (XF-61). To be realistic, the paler colour of the camouflage would in reality be painted last and not as thickly as the base, so that after a long

time in combat it would peel away and the base colour appear through instead. The worn paintwork cannot be made entirely at random: chips are the distinct consequence of certain effects — such as driving through stony terrain — and have an irregular but repeated appearance.

Mud

In some photos, the wheels of the vehicles appear with semi-dry mud encrusted between their treads; in the areas where there is less mud it is already almost dry. This dry mud is undoubtedly much paler than the wet mud, and the wet, as well as being shinier, is darker. This is why we imitated it with putty and sand, painting the dry mud first with buff (XF-57) and white using an airbrush. Then, with a brush we painted the fresh mud with matt earth (XF-52), following this with a wash of 75 percent gloss varnish, 10 percent turpentine and paint thinner and 15 percent chocolate

The tank is completed with the figures of the crew, suitably painted and adapted to suit the style of the model.

The greatest tonal variety of colours must be used, particularly in the flatter and less detailed areas of the model.

The accessories and equipment always give the model more realism and make it more striking.

brown. On the face of the wheels in direct contact with the caterpillar, leave the natural colour of the rubber as it would be completely cleaned by the friction.

Complementary elements

Unable to discover what colour the lateral grids should be, we decided to paint them in a different tone to the rest of the tank, as though the crew could not be bothered to camouflage them. As regards such homely details as the mattress: although it seems strange, in the same book there are vehicles with blankets and mattresses tied with straps. Judging by recent photos of the war in Chechnya, it is common for the Russian Army to have blankets and mattresses on board with them.

BIBLIOGRAPHY

Armor of the Afghanistan War, Concord.
T-54, T-55, T-62, Concord.
Tank War-Central Front Nato vs Warsaw Pact, Concord.

Croatian T-34/85

During the Balkan War, the conflicting groups needed to distinguish captured vehicles and materials as their own. They achieved this by means of gaudy and, in most cases, entirely useless camouflage. In addition, soldiers frequently painted inscriptions on these vehicles with the initials of their countries or leaders.

In the Balkan conflict, soldiers on the front lines had to rely on their own creativity or copy any stray pictorial material they found in the towns to paint their tanks. Of course, whatever colours could be found were used and applied in many different ways. In fact, it can be said that there were as many camouflages as there were vehicles and 'artists'. Although it is impossible to organise and classify these camouflages in terms of geography or period, there are some that stand out for their originality and others because they include elements that appear on a number of vehicles. For example, soldiers although in different places

The wheels of this T-34/85 belong to a T-55 tank.

An original detail is the Browning machine gun mounted on the turret.

would find sprays of the same colour (primer, orange, black, blue, etc.) with which to paint their tanks. This, in turn, gave rise to camouflages using the same colours, albeit differently patterned and applied.

Also, the creative capacity of the soldiers at the front was usually similarly reflected in their camouflages, though using different colours; that is to say, it is very unlikely that many of the combatants would have attempted a camouflage using cloud shapes (since it would be harder to do) but there would be concurrence in the use of lightning shapes which are easily made with spray cans, and characteristic of people with little artistic ability. Therefore, most of the camouflages in the Balkans have irregular and unsightly paint jobs. Also, the distribution of the colour over

the tank is uneven. If they could not reach an area, it would be left unpainted or if they ran out of colour, it would be left unfinished or changed to another.

This information is important when we work on our model, since we want it look realistic and not amateurish as with a model painted by a beginner.

Lettering

Vehicles were frequently painted with identifying names, although on many occasions the words written on the tanks tended to be more personal slogans. The Slovenians, for example, painted most of their captured vehicles with the initials TO, *Teritorialna Obramada* (territorial army) in white. The Croatians put the initials ZNG (JNA) on their vehicles and the Bosnians BiH (*Bosnia i Herzegovina*), but occasionally they wrote the names of their loved ones or home towns, and some vehicles even appear with nicknames, such as 'U2', 'Bomba' or 'Alf'.

However, all the paint jobs were characterised by their sloppy execution and clashing colours, such as ultramarine, yellow or vermilion. So, don't paint on these names beautifully or use transfers, but rather do it apparently roughly, leaving the letters irregular and blurred.

Although we can appreciate all these points on the vehicles in the photos, it is much more difficult to interpret them on a scale model. As modellers we have eyes and hands that are too accustomed to making camouflage perfect!

For this reason, we must think a little like the creators of these camouflages. They certainly did not stop to think about the aesthetics or the final finish.

It is necessary, then, to produce bold, confident camouflage, even though they look quite bad and amateurish, since the effects of dust and wear will make the model look lifelike and realistic in the end.

The Croatian T-34

For this experiment, we started with several photographs from the Concord book *The Balkans on Fire*, which illustrated some T-34s modified by Croat soldiers after capturing them from the enemy. This tank, although obsolete by the time of the Croatian war, the T-34 served as mobile artillery and was used to destroy small vehicles, although its participation was not very significant. In the eyes of a model maker, it can be attractive to model on account of its unique modifications.

The tank is equipped with the modern wheels of the Russian T-55 and its headlights. More surprising is the ersatz placing of a 12.7mm (0.50in.) Browning

on the rear section of the turret, which is protected by boxes of American or Russian ammunition, like those carried by the Dushka. This does not seem very believable at first sight, but is logical considering that the former Yugoslavian army had Western as well as Asian armaments.

Another important point is the change in the base colour. The original Soviet green (very dark) was painted over with the new and much paler Yugoslavian green; this was then extended to the whole fleet of vehicles. On top of the tank, their regulation numbers were originally painted in white. Once captured by the Croats, another phase began.

With a good selection of sprays and tins of colour paint seized in the towns, the Croats camouflaged the whole tank without any consistent approach — with the only limits being the quantity of colours obtained. The order and shapes are usually completely random, although they

Various accessories to give the vehicle a setting, standing out among which is this container.

sometimes put something premeditated, as we can see on the camouflage chart. They also sometimes left areas unpainted, either because they ran out of the colour or because they did not consider it important. In our case, the rear was not camouflaged and neither was the front of the barrel. Although they used colours that were not very military, be careful to interpret them to scale, since in reality these bright colours would have been affected by the bad weather and wear and tear.

Our artist has a used special camouflage of squiggles in two tones: one medium red like metal primer, and one yellow. When doing the lines, make sure they are the correct thickness, and characteristic of a spray to our scale.

CAMOUFLAGE CHART

In the following chart are a series of camouflages chosen for their originality or their extensive use; they are only a small part of those that can be seen in the books *The Balkans at War* and *The Balkans on Fire*, both published by Concord.

1. Camouflage using spray gun and brown colour on a military green base. It was finished off with an orange spray and points of black. Letters were outlined with a fine brush.
2. Typical decoration of vehicles captured by elite troops in Osijek. Strips of brown in the style of giraffes, with fillers in black and specks of bluish sand. The emblems were perfectly labelled in white.
3. General dirtying of a vehicle with various colours and different degrees of paintwork decay. Irregular brushstrokes in black, green, brown and orange. Without a doubt, a real challenge for the model maker as it is more daring and unpleasant for the poor scale model.
4. Camouflage-lettering. Often the soldiers that captured tanks quickly daubed the more visible parts in black to distinguish them from those of the enemy, although it is not impossible that they later decorated them much better.
5. This is perhaps the most widespread camouflage in the Croatian lines; brown with large markings and fine yellow lines served to support large and distinctive brushed letters.
6. Camouflage on military green. This type was composed of enormous areas of pale yellowish green overlaid with fine quick strokes of black.
7. Original painting formed with small clouds of sand colour and black stripes. Possibly only appeared on one BDRM 2 in the whole war.
8. There was always some expert who was able to make a camouflage that really camouflaged, as we can see in this example taken from a T-55 in Dubrovnik. Black and dark green on a green base. Letters in white or dark blue.
9. Another popular and widespread design. Orange and black spray winding irregularly across the vehicle, with letters in blue or red.
10. This camouflage deserves special attention (although it is possibly the only one in the entire Balkans). As we can see, it is a camouflage executed by somebody who is an expert in military history, specifically from World War I. The outline and colours are typical of that time and have also been finished off with a identifiable German cross. Very original and simple to to do, although in fact it is painted with little precision.
11. This is the winner for originality. A decoration using all the spray cans the soldiers could get. Zigzags of lawn green, red, orange, blue, etc.
12. Another good attempt at camouflage using yellow and brown spray. These strips were well planned and well constructed.

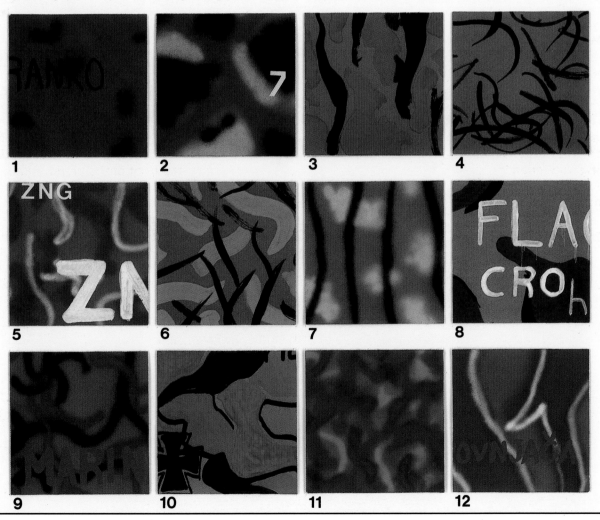

The wording distributed over the tank was done by hand with a brush and with other tins of different colours. If it was painful to paint the vehicle with these peculiar colours, it is even more so to paint it with these horrible letters over the whole chassis! But just remind yourself that later the setting will unify and give realism to the whole thing.

Finally, it must also be emphasised that usually the bottom parts of most of the tanks and trucks were not painted.

Dirtying the model realistically is perhaps the most difficult job, since it is necessary to think of something that does not become just another colour. In this case, we opted for a dry whitish mud, characteristic of the soils around Dubrovnik. But remember that mud can be any number of colours, from greys to browns, to reds and blacks.

The effects of dry mud are shown all over the tank, giving a characteristic whitish appearance.

This mud, which turned into dust when dried out by the sun, impregnates the whole vehicle, giving the whole thing a whitish cast; but due to the activity of its crew, cleaner and glossier areas must appear where they touch the vehicle. I'm not giving colour references, as such a variety of dusts and camouflages exists that it would be an endless process to name them one by one. Suffice to say that almost any colour can be used for vehicles in this conflict. It is the concepts outlined here that are much more important.

The chippings are another fundamental part of the finish, although we will only apply a couple of types of rust and dark green as they were on the original Russian green.

Finally, we applied the rest of the effects typical of any tank, such as grease, spilled water and gasoline, splashes of mud, uncovered metal and so on.

The tracks of dry mud have been reproduced on the asphalt.

The Scene

To frame this atypical T-34 in context, I have surrounded it with elements of its time and place. Taking my cue from some photos, I included some dustbins filled with rubbish and glass. The aluminium one was made from scratch, copying ones found around our streets. The glass one was more difficult, but I started with a deodorant lid that exactly fits the actual scale measurements. It was completed with pieces of plastic card and decorated with the appropriate colours.

A street light provides a strong vertical which all dioramas need, and of course the road must be appropriately distressed to show where the tank has gouged its caterpillar tracks into the asphalt, leaving it as dusty as the tank.

Merkava — Wear in the Desert

There are many methods and types of painting that can be used on models of tanks operating in the desert. The spectacular Merkava is an armoured vehicle that is ideal for recreating all kinds of effects, in this case highlighting the more unusual use of pastel colours.

Among model makers, there has been much discussion about Israeli combat tanks and their exact colours. The best thing to do is to study all the available documentation as closely as possible. It is also necessary to know how to interpret the colouring, to observe its effects and note how well it merges into the environment or how it looks when in combat on the terrain.

Modern Israeli vehicles and tanks are basically painted in a greyish colour, the exact tone of which is remarkably difficult to get right, so we decided to apply a paint base composed of the following mixture: 16 percent dark grey (XF-24), 34 percent buff colour (XF-57), 8 percent sky blue (XF-21), 8 percent light blue (XF-23), 18 percent olive green (XF-58) and finally 16 percent earth (XF-52); all these are acrylics from Tamiya. Once this primer tone was dry, we varnished the model with a gloss finish and then marked on the grooves, nuts and bolts and other such details with oil washes or black enamel.

The effect of dust on the front part of the upper hull. The dust was obtained from ground chalk which provides colour and texture at the same time.

The biggest problem that arises with chalk is the difficulty in fixing the powder pigment so that it will stay on the surface of the vehicle.

The vehicles belonging to the Israeli Army suffer an almost unique deterioration due to such extreme environments, such as the heat and dust of the Negev desert and the humidity and cold that are typical of the Golan Heights — both areas in which the IDF habitually operate. Added to this is the slow but constant deterioration of knocks and bumps due to use by the crews, the transportation of all kinds of goods and equipment, etc. The result of all this activity are the chippings, friction marks, dents, dinks and other damage.

In the specific case of paint chips, a graphite grey colour has been used to imitate the most extreme ones and sky blue (XF-21) for simple scratches. These are distributed over the model, as we can see in the photos, always keeping in mind their tendency to appear in the parts most exposed to friction. Lastly, a small touch of metallic grey (XF–56) is added to some areas, toning down later with dark grey (XF-24) to prevent it from being too obvious.

Close scrutiny will also show reddish stains on the metal mainly around the fuel intakes, this is caused by the mixture of gasoline and the reddish desert dust during refuelling. This effect is imitated by airbrushing in an orange-brown colour. The airbrush is in turn used to reproduce bits of earth and dry mud that have stuck mainly to the underside and wheels. The required tone is a mix of matt earth (XF-52) and reddish brown (XF-64). The spattering of muddy water has been done by brush with the colour buff (XF-57).

On the underside extra ageing has been shown by means of enamel washes with khaki (no. 26) and sand (no. 187, both from Humbrol), together with natural sienna earth and yellow ochre with oil. With this mixture we managed to simulate the effect of splashes of water on the dust accumulated in the lower area of the tank, which produce evaporation and drying marks.

The Effects of Dust

This is a technical question that deserves to be dealt with separately, because it is the

most interesting part of the ageing process. One of the most striking aspects when observing photos of these tanks operating in the desert is the simply enormous quantity of dust that accumulates on all the surfaces, occasionally even completely concealing the base colour. It can even give the impression that these are deliberate coats of paint, as though it were a camouflage.

To create a feeling of the clogging, all-pervasive dust, we used powdered coloured chalk. The biggest inconvenience with this is that in time the dusty effect created with the chalk tends to disappear — the bonus though is that chalk gives a very realistic finish. First scrape the correct coloured chalk with the edge of a knife or a piece of sandpaper making the powder as fine as possible; discard any small pieces that break off. Then, with a no. 5 or 6 paintbrush, pick up the powder and spread it over the model, gently tapping the paintbrush with the index finger so the powder falls off.

As evenly as possible extend the chalk dust over the required area. When sufficiently covered, touch it up lightly with the tip of the paintbrush to fix it. Gently blow away excess powder. Then, with a clean paintbrush, rub the dust softly as though working with the dry brush technique, in order to blend it into a uniform covering. You may find it necessary to repeat this operation several times on the same part of the model to get the necessary intensity.

Armament

Although it seems exaggerated, the photos show that the weapons also get very dirty; their parts covered with the reddish dust of the desert stand out, giving them an interesting rusty appearance.

Close-up showing the amount of detailing with hatches and equipment as well as the distribution of dust and grime.

Whatever the effect of reproducing dirt and wear, it must always be perfectly blended and integrated with the other colours, effects and textures, in order to produce a believable degree of uniformity.

Insignia

Israeli armoured vehicles have an attractive identification system — generally, it consists of a white 'V' that indicates the number of the battalion, depending on the position in which it is placed. A Hebrew letter and a figure indicate respectively the number of the platoon and the vehicle's number within it. This code may appear painted on the same tank or on a piece of canvas that the crew fix on the sides of the turret.

In some tanks there may also be a white fringe painted lengthways on the barrel — this is used for aerial identification. These fringes are usually crossed by others of the same colour, with their number or distribution varying from one tank to the next. To help aerial identification, there are also fluorescent orange tarpaulins. Sometimes names are painted on in Hebrew, referring to the name of the tank given by the crew, or some other appropriate slogan.

BIBLIOGRAPHY

The three books used as reference are: *Merkava I, II, III, Israel Armor Might* and *Battleground Lebanon*. They are all published by Concord.